PACIFIC TRANSPORT SECTOR ASSESSMENT, STRATEGY, AND ROAD MAP 2021–2025

JULY 2021

ASIAN DEVELOPMENT BANK

ADB

Notes:
In this publication, "$" refers to United States dollars.
All photos in this publications are from ADB.

On the cover: Aerial shot of Western Highlands Province, Papua New Guinea (photo by ADB).
Cover design by Jan Carlo del Cruz.

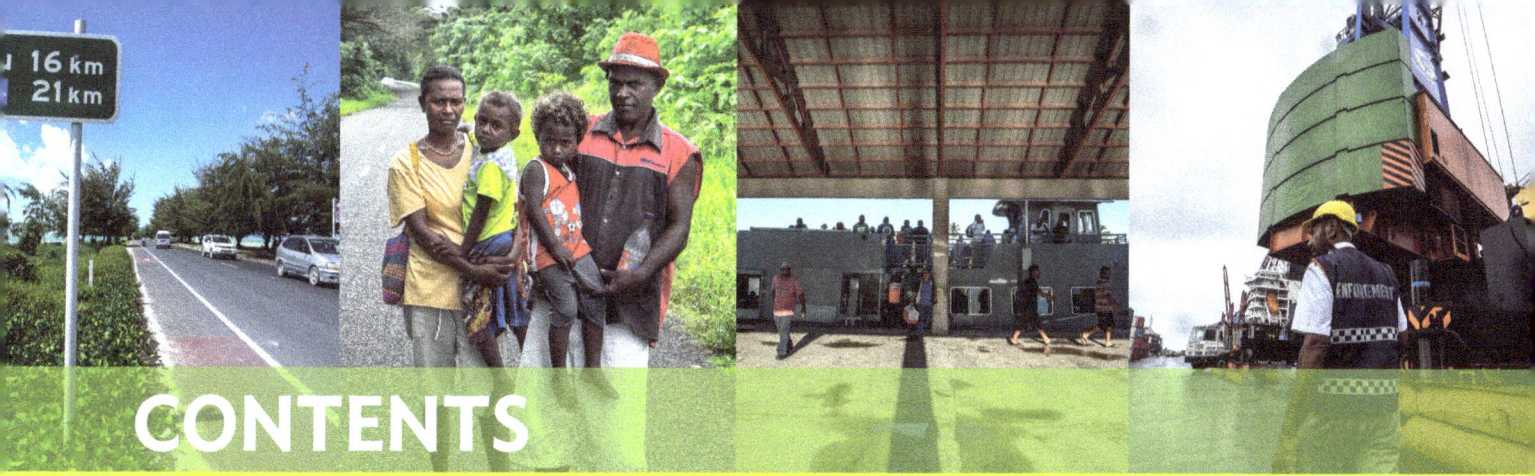

CONTENTS

FOREWORD

The 14 Pacific developing member countries (DMCs) of the Asian Development Bank (ADB) are scattered across 30 million square kilometers of ocean, with a total population of 10 million people. The Pacific DMCs are geographically dispersed and isolated from international markets; experience acute connectivity constraints; and are highly vulnerable to external shocks, including natural hazards and the effects of climate change.

ADB partners with governments, communities, and the private sector to improve access to essential goods, services, and opportunities. Operations in the region are enhancing connectivity and building resilience to external shocks through improved services and infrastructure—including maritime, aviation, land transport, and urban mobility systems.

The Transport Sector Assessment, Strategy, and Road Map provides an overview of and strategic directions for ADB's transport sector operations in targeting an ambitious 5-year transport pipeline and associated implementation approaches in the Pacific DMCs. ADB's transport strategy for the Pacific DMCs is based on domestic and regional sector priorities, and ADB's Strategy 2030.

ADB's transport strategy for the Pacific will help tackle core development challenges by focusing on improving connectivity, developing livable cities, and delivering support to address climate change and enhance resilience. Transport sector support in the region will also foster deeper regional cooperation and integration to promote inclusive economic growth. ADB will continue to support local governments to improve their business environments, and increasingly help structure public–private partnerships to deliver sustainable transport services.

ADB's transport operations will continue to address the different needs of men and women, and populations in both outer islands and urban centers—seeking to deliver socioeconomic benefits through increased access to employment, markets, education, and health services.

The Transport Sector Assessment, Strategy, and Road Map is linked to and informs ADB's strategy document for the region, the Pacific Approach—both documents cover the period from 2021 to 2025.

Leah C. Gutierrez

Leah C. Gutierrez
Director General, Pacific Department
Asian Development Bank

ACKNOWLEDGMENTS

This report aims to assess the transport sector in the Pacific and to operationalize the transport sector work in the region of the Asian Development Bank (ADB) in the context of ADB's Strategy 2030. Ari Kalliokoski, senior transport economist, led the preparation of the report. Leah Gutierrez, director general, and Dong Kyu Lee, director, Transport and Communications Division, Pacific Department (PARD), provided overall guidance and advice. The report also benefited from inputs by Rustam Ishenaliev, principal infrastructure specialist; Sibesh Bhattacharya, principal infrastructure specialist (ICT); Syed Hussain Haider, senior transport specialist; Cha-Sang Shim, transport specialist; Tomoaki Kawabata, transport specialist; Juan Gonzalez Jimenez, transport specialist; and Roble Velasco-Rosenheim, ADB consultant. Cecilia Caparas, associate knowledge management officer, PARD, and Raymond De Vera, senior operations assistant, Energy Division, Central and West Asia Department, coordinated the publishing process. This guide was edited by Ricardo Chan and Lawrence Casiraya, and layout and design was executed by Rommel Marilla.

SECTOR ASSESSMENT: CONTEXT AND STRATEGIC ISSUES

A major road in Tarawa, Kiribati.

Introduction

This assessment, strategy, and road map (ASR) provides an overview of the transport sector in the Pacific developing member countries (DMCs) of the Asian Development Bank (ADB).[1] The ASR highlights sector performance; priority development constraints; and ADB's support, experience, and strategic directions for the transport sector in its Pacific DMCs. The ASR is linked to and informs ADB's strategy document for the region, the Pacific Approach.[2] Both the ASR and the Pacific Approach cover the period from 2021 to 2025.

ADB's 14 Pacific DMCs are scattered across 30 million square kilometers of ocean or one-third of the earth's surface, but their combined landmass represents less than 2% of this total. They are isolated from international markets and highly vulnerable to the effects of climate change. The remote, archipelagic geography of most Pacific DMCs, paired with their small and dispersed populations, creates a unique set of challenges for connecting people, goods, and services. At the same time, the Pacific DMCs are highly dependent on trade. The majority of their goods are imported—including food, fuel, and medicine—while mineral and fish exports, alongside tourism and remittances, underpin economic growth. Connectivity infrastructure is essential for helping the Pacific DMCs to lower the costs of trade, safeguard against climate risks and economic volatility, and create value through deeper interaction in global markets.

Subsector Issues and Lessons

Maritime transport. Ports and wharves are an essential lifeline for communities across the Pacific. Small wharves and jetties connect people on the outer islands to resources and opportunities in cities, while larger commercial ports are the primary gateway to international trade. Safe and resilient wharves and jetties increase accessibility to remote and isolated areas; and more efficient ports reduce transport costs, encourage exports, and can scale up transshipment economies in a number of the Pacific DMCs. Upgrading physical infrastructure and strengthening institutional capacity are also essential for increasing resilience to natural disasters and the effects of climate change, and enhancing maritime safety.

Aviation. The aviation industry in the Pacific can play a vital role in the changing economic and social development of the Pacific DMCs by promoting tourism, agriculture, and social cohesion. There is significant unrealized potential for civil aviation to support national development. However, the Pacific aviation environment is challenging, with a history of substandard and unsafe infrastructure, an ageing fleet, low rural connectivity, and weak policy and regulatory frameworks.

Land transport. Roads are the backbone of the Pacific transport sector, and are major drivers of more inclusive economic growth. They are essential for connecting rural populations to basic goods and services, increasing access to domestic market opportunities, and facilitating the movement of goods

---

[1]   ADB's 14 Pacific DMCs are the Cook Islands, Fiji, Kiribati, the Marshall Islands, the Federated States of Micronesia, Nauru, Niue, Palau, Papua New Guinea, Samoa, Solomon Islands, Tonga, Tuvalu, and Vanuatu.

[2]   The Pacific Approach serves as ADB's country partnership strategy and operational framework for the 12 small Pacific island countries, or the "PIC-12". The PIC 12 comprise all of the Pacific DMCs, excluding Fiji and Papua New Guinea, which have their own individual country partnership strategies.

from production sites onward to ports and airports for export. Although many Pacific DMCs have (or once had) adequate transport infrastructure, limited resource allocations have led to the accelerated degradation of key assets, and roads in particular. Further, road crash and fatality rates are high in the Pacific, when compared to international standards.

Urban mobility. The rapid influx of people into urban centers and peri-urban areas threatens to strain transport and mobility in urban areas. This challenge is compounded by rising incomes, which is leading to an increase in the motor vehicle fleet. Uncontrolled growth in urban road traffic and associated congestion is compromising the health and safety of urban dwellers in the Pacific's larger cities.

Intermodal connectivity. Intermodal transport links can help the Pacific DMCs bridge physical and economic gaps domestically, regionally, and internationally. Effective ports, roads, and airports can increase access to markets and opportunities, thereby minimizing the rural–urban divide and expanding access to essential goods and services. At the same time, improving transport efficiency can reduce the costs of conducing trade, and accessing goods and services.

Thematic Issues and Lessons

Climate change adaptation and disaster risk management. In global disaster risk indices, Pacific countries such as Palau, Solomon Islands, Tonga, and Vanuatu are consistently ranked among the 10 most-at-risk countries in the world. Natural hazards, compounded by the effects of climate change, are producing frequent and tangible losses in the Pacific region. Disaster events, such as tropical cyclones, have grown in intensity; while heightened weather variability is leading to prolonged periods of drought

The Aiwo boat harbor in Nauru.

and flooding. Sea level rise, spring tides and storm surges, and other extreme events associated with climate change can have devastating effects on connectivity infrastructure.

Regional cooperation and integration. The Pacific DMCs face deeper barriers to trade than most countries in the world. Distance from major markets increases the costs of goods and services, while limited capacity and transport infrastructure restrict logistics and trade efficiency. However, the location of Pacific DMCs along major maritime trade routes creates significant opportunities to establish their role as transshipment hubs.

Gender. Women and girls face a number of barriers to accessing the benefits of transport systems in the Pacific. These barriers include time poverty, family-caring responsibilities, limited decision-making power, economic status, and concerns relating to safety such as gender-based violence. All of these obstacles inform women's travel patterns, access to modes of transport, and utilization of transport infrastructure and services. There is also a lack of women employed in decision-making positions in the transport sector, and women's concerns and preferences are often overlooked in transport planning. Transport investments that take into account the different needs of men and women in the Pacific can bring significant socioeconomic benefits as women have increased access to employment, markets, education, and health services.

Institutional and capacity constraints. Most Pacific economies have thin institutional capacities, which is reflected in constraints to staffing and resourcing of government systems given the high turnover of staff, and small human resource pools and economic bases. Many borrowers in the Pacific lack the

Schoolchildren waiting for their transport near Kings Road, Suva, Fiji.

capacity to prepare projects without support. The project management agencies in the transport sector often lack experienced staff to efficiently manage projects throughout the project cycle.

Landownership. Ownership structures in the Pacific are often complex, involving varying practices of customary tenure linked to social and traditional belief systems. Land acquisition for transport projects can be particularly time-consuming, especially for linear infrastructure projects involving multiple land parcels and groups of customary landowners and private interests. The remoteness of project locations and challenging terrain add to the difficulties; in some countries, the history of colonization and insufficiently resourced government institutions have resulted in poor land records and residual legacy issues. The associated difficulties with acquiring land can impact the efficiency of project implementation.

Procurement. Isolation of Pacific DMCs often limits the number of active qualified contractors in the region. The main challenges involve isolation and diseconomies of scale; remoteness leads to high cost structures for implementation, while the relatively small contract values in the region are insufficient to attract large qualified bidders. At the same time, lack of specialized skills in domestic labor markets can increase challenges associated with staffing infrastructure projects and ensuring that domestic entities provide long-term maintenance. Procurement challenges—paired with mountainous terrain, atoll topography, and in some cases even unexploded ordinances—can lead to cost- and time-overruns, or require projects to close without reaching completion. These challenges complicate procurement and can jeopardize project sustainability.

II SECTOR STRATEGY

A family walking along a road on the outskirts of Honiara, Solomon Islands.

Government Sector Strategies

Although there is significant diversity across countries in the Pacific, many DMCs face a similar set of connectivity challenges in the transport sector. ADB works with DMC governments, individually, to support them in developing country-specific strategies, but also with key regional bodies, such as the Secretariat of the Pacific Community, or with regional coordination initiatives, such as the Pacific Region Infrastructure Facility (PRIF). ADB is helping the Pacific DMCs to uncover regional challenges and pool resources to address them. Some of the key thematic areas include:

Building resilience to climate change and disasters. Adaptation and risk-reduction measures required to increase the resilience of infrastructure can involve significant incremental costs on top of the underlying infrastructure investments. In addition to resilience-oriented spatial planning and design standards, transport systems require investments in risk-informed asset management. Further, transport agencies need to respond rapidly to restore critical routes during and after hazard events. Strengthening the resilience of transport systems in the region requires the capacity to assess, coordinate, and mobilize resources; and the ability to rapidly contract for the recovery of damaged infrastructure, all while balancing the need to "build back better", that is, ensuring that new assets are designed to higher resilience standards than the damaged ones.

Promoting tourism to build economies. The idyllic landscapes and pristine natural environments across the Pacific have drawn tourists to the region for decades. However, limited connectivity infrastructure leads to high costs of travel and difficulty reaching the more remote parts of the Pacific DMCs. Scaling up the tourism industry is contingent on increased intermodal transport links. Governments across the region are focusing on building the corresponding infrastructure and increasing tourism receipts as key drivers of growth.

Providing connectivity to populations in remote areas. Physical isolation is a persistent challenge for populations across the region. This is true particularly for the people living in outer islands or in mountainous parts of the Pacific DMCs. Governments across the region are targeting increased connectivity to support socioeconomic inclusion. National transport strategies identify ways to promulgate commercially viable transport services, while building rural roads, wharves and jetties, and airstrips to the least-connected areas. Doing so is key to increasing access to resources and opportunities.

Promoting private sector growth and sector sustainability. While financing physical connectivity in the Pacific is typically not financially viable for the private sector, legislative and financial reforms in the transport sector need to be continued to improve the business environment and support the sector's long-term financial sustainability. Reforming state-owned enterprises and creating public–private partnerships, for instance, can assist DMC objectives in reducing the costs of doing business and delivering transport services, and promote growth led by the private sector.

Promoting rural development. Agriculture and fishing have a vast potential in Pacific DMCs, but businesses in these industries in the region are typically unorganized and conducted on a small scale. Farmers and fishers face common challenges that include lack of access to finance, low yields, lack of storage and market infrastructure, limited local value addition, and dependence on brokers. ADB's transport projects will provide improved access to markets and services that will be further strengthened with social and poverty components that provide technical skills training and physical market and storage facilities.

Supporting social inclusive transport. Designing social-inclusive and gender-responsive transport and infrastructure requires meaningful and early engagement and consultation with all stakeholder groups, including women and girls. Lack of sex-disaggregated data and gender-sensitive transport surveys and studies pose a challenge to ensuring appropriate and inclusive project designs. To leverage the benefits of inclusive transport infrastructure, consideration should be given also to supporting services to meet the needs of women and girls and other vulnerable user groups, such as transport timetables and preventive measures to reduce gender-based violence and improve accessibility in public transport.

Development Partners and Collaboration

ADB's key development partners in the Pacific transport sector include bilateral donors such as the governments of Australia, the People's Republic of China, Japan, New Zealand, and the broader European Union. Major multilateral partners include the United Nations and the World Bank. ADB is also working with international climate resources, including the Green Climate Fund, to help its Pacific DMCs access finance to support transport infrastructure that mitigates the causes of climate change and helps build resilience to disaster events. ADB is the key partner of the Pacific Private Sector Development Initiative (PSDI), which is a regional technical assistance (TA) program to alleviate poverty and promote

Funafuti International Airport in Tuvalu.

economic growth in the Pacific region through reforms that reduce the constraints to doing business and promote inclusive growth, entrepreneurship, and new business models.[3] ADB is also a founding member of PRIF—a coordination mechanism between partners, which focuses on development of the economic infrastructure in Pacific.[4]

ADB coordinates its investments and TA closely with development partners to ensure that individual projects complement each other, and to identify cofinancing opportunities. The typically high cost and complexity of transport projects in the region has encouraged a higher degree of collaboration among development partners than in almost any other global region. For example, the Pacific is the only region in the world where ADB and the World Bank cofinance projects as opposed to delivering finance in parallel. ADB's use of sector lending has encouraged it to work closely with national governments to pool development partner resources into transport funds that deliver long-term impacts.

ADB Strategy 2030

Improving connectivity in the Pacific supports each of the seven pillars of ADB's Strategy 2030.[5] Connectivity projects contribute to the broader strategy by

Addressing remaining poverty and reducing inequalities by increasing access to opportunities and providing jobs in the formal economy. ADB transport operations engage communities and local contractors to bridge skills gaps across the Pacific—increasing opportunities for gainful employment and deepening the social impacts of investments.

Accelerating progress in gender equality by fostering more equitable participation in the workforce and supporting women to participate in decision-making roles. ADB requires gender-sensitive designs in the tendered projects, which is helping deepen engagement of local female workers in infrastructure works and increased opportunities for women to find meaningful employment.

Tackling climate change, building climate and disaster resilience, and enhancing environmental sustainability by designing and constructing transport infrastructure that is more resilient to severe weather events, building human and institutional capacity to manage and respond to disasters, and assisting countries to react to natural hazards with a "build back better" approach.

---

[3] Other key partners are the Government of Australia and the Government of New Zealand.
[4] Other key partners are the Australian Department of Foreign Affairs and Trade, the New Zealand Ministry of Foreign Affairs and Trade, the World Bank Group, the European Commission, the European Investment Bank, and the Japan International Cooperation Agency.
[5] ADB. 2018. *Strategy 2030: Achieving a Prosperous, Inclusive, Resilient, and Sustainable Asia and the Pacific.* Manila.

Making cities more livable by improving urban mobility and addressing interlinked health and safety concerns. Projects and technical assistance are (i) building government capacity to plan and manage the growth of cities and peri-urban areas; (ii) constructing evacuation routes to strengthen disaster resilience; and (iii) improving roads alongside other key urban infrastructure, including footpaths, sewerage, and drainage.

Promoting rural development and food security by connecting rural populations to the resources they need to thrive. ADB transport operations in the Pacific are financing (i) maritime links between cities and populations on outer islands, (ii) airports and runways to link remote communities to essential goods like food and medicine, and (iii) transnational road infrastructure that connects communities to key resources and economic opportunities.

Strengthening governance and institutional capacity by training local stakeholders to plan and implement investments, and to manage and maintain transport infrastructure sustainably. By engaging local governments, businesses, and communities, ADB is supporting its Pacific DMCs to increase the physical and financial sustainability of their transport sectors.

Fostering regional cooperation and integration by improving transport infrastructure and trade logistics to reduce the cost of doing business, increase access to international markets, and support economic growth at the regional and national levels. ADB's Pacific transport operations are helping to identify specific trade bottlenecks and working with stakeholders across sectors to overcome them.

III ADB SECTOR EXPERIENCE AND APPROACH

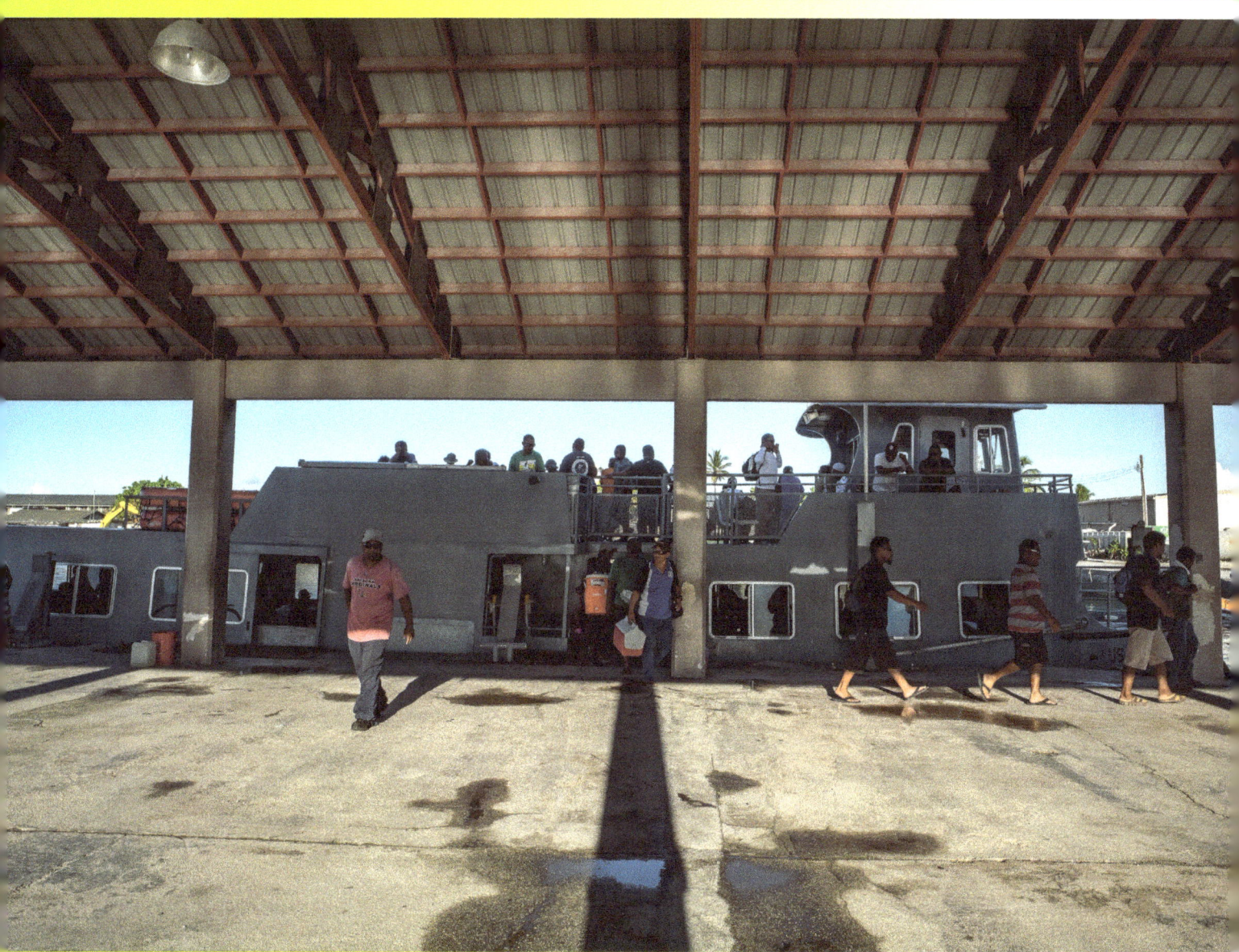

Passenger ferry services in Ebeye, Marshall Islands.

Guided by ADB's Strategy 2030 and Pacific Approach, operations in the Pacific transport sector seek to (i) prepare for and respond to shocks, (ii) deliver sustainable services, and (iii) support inclusive growth in all of the Pacific DMCs. The region's unique geography, sociopolitical structures, and economic context require a specialized approach to designing and implementing projects. ADB's operations in the Pacific transport sector build on 5 decades of experience supporting unique regional circumstances.

Sector Experience

ADB has been active in the Pacific transport sector since 1972, making it one of the first development partners to support connectivity in the region. Through its long-standing support, ADB has helped identify a number of region-specific constraints and has developed a series of approaches to help the Pacific DMCs overcome them.

ADB is supporting the Pacific DMCs to plan, build, and maintain their connectivity infrastructure. Transport projects account for more than 59% of the total value of ADB's portfolio in the Pacific. ADB's transport portfolio comprised 17 projects valued at more than $1.4 billion at the end of 2019, with an additional 27 projects valued at $2.3 billion in the pipeline for 2020–2023. ADB's support for the transport sector is bridging gaps to drive more prosperous, inclusive, resilient, and sustainable growth in the Pacific region.

Maritime

ADB is supporting maritime transport with physical investments alongside capacity building. ADB is supporting Nauru to upgrade the main commercial port in Aiwo, which will strengthen its resilience to climate change, increase its port capacity, and improve the efficiency of its port operations. Planned projects in Apia (Samoa), Nuku'alofa (Tonga), as well as Honiara (Solomon Islands) will upgrade the existing ports to increase vessel and transshipment capacity, while significantly improving safety, security, and climate resilience. ADB's investments in commercial ports are deepening regional cooperation and integration to support economic growth, and reducing the cost of goods and services for people across the Pacific.

ADB is also helping to reduce poverty and inequality and promote rural development by upgrading maritime transport assets on remote islands. Upgrading rural wharves and jetties increases access to markets and opportunities while enhancing the safety of people and goods.

Sector lending in Fiji and Solomon Islands is supporting the respective governments to improve connectivity between the outer islands and major urban centers, with a focus on more resilient docking facilities. Projects in Kiribati, Papua New Guinea, Tuvalu, and Vanuatu are improving remote maritime infrastructure alongside navigation and safety equipment. Complementary capacity building for maritime safety organizations and private ship operators is improving the security of passengers and goods, and increasing the frequency of interisland transport services.

Aviation

Since 2010, ADB has supported Papua New Guinea to rehabilitate and upgrade national airports to develop safe, effective, and reliable aviation services. Investments have focused on ground-side improvements such as strengthening and extending runways, navigational safety, and security fencing. Capacity building is helping the government to plan and manage future investments in the aviation sector, and to achieve compliance with standards set by the Civil Aviation Safety Authority (CASA) of Papua New Guinea.[6] In the next phase, ADB will build on an ongoing program by linking national airports with all-weather rural airstrips, institutional development, and capacity development of aviation sector agencies.

Programmatic lending in Papua New Guinea has helped provide a long-term vision for its aviation subsector and is improving safety conditions and operations in 22 national airports. The program is also building the capacity of domestic stakeholders to manage and maintain all assets.

Land Transport

Since 2010, ADB has helped its Pacific DMCs construct or upgrade 1,032 kilometers of roads, while ongoing projects will construct additional 1,173 kilometers by 2022. Upgrading road networks and providing regular maintenance extend their economic life, and create opportunities for local businesses and communities to engage in the development process. ADB is helping its Pacific DMCs to overcome the "build, neglect, rebuild" paradigm by focusing on the sustainable management of road networks.

Safety is also a key area for ADB's loans and grants in the road subsector. Improved safety furniture, such as signage, guardrails, street markings, and walkways, is helping reduce crashes and enhance the safety of pedestrians. By including roadside market structures, bus stops, safe access to fresh water sources, and better lighting in its road projects, ADB is helping increase economic opportunities for women in rural communities, and enhancing the safety of women and girls. Several road maintenance measures are being considered to ensure the sustainability of investments, including maintenance programs that use the local workforce.

Urban Mobility

ADB takes a comprehensive approach to developing livable cities. Urban development projects in the Pacific DMCs take a holistic approach to asset construction and maintenance, ensuring that road infrastructure is adequate to avoid traffic congestion, and that roadside drainage is built to high resilience standards. ADB's support for livable cities engages municipal and national governments to ensure that growing urban centers provide safe and resilient transport, alongside essential water and sanitation services.

---

[6]   CASA is a statutory body with a legal mandate to promote safety and security in Papua New Guinea's civil aviation system. As a signatory to the Convention of International Civil Aviation, CASA is responsible for ensuring sustained domestic compliance with international civil safety standards.

Urban development projects in the Pacific are also helping address key risks associated with climate change. For example, in Samoa, ADB is upgrading a central cross island road that will reduce traffic congestion to and from the nation's capital, while providing access and livelihoods to inland communities. In Vanuatu, ADB helped build government capacity to manage urban sprawl and the development of informal settlements, while constructing roads, improving drainage to protect against flooding, and increasing access to safe water and sanitation. ADB's support for cities is helping improve living standards in urban and peri-urban areas, as populations across the region migrate to find new jobs and opportunities.

Climate Change and Resilience

ADB is supporting Pacific DMCs in key sectors to respond to the immense and growing adaptation needs in the region. This includes scaling up analysis of the risks associated with natural hazards (including climate change-related hazards) to inform spatial planning and adaptation pathways for the Pacific DMCs. Informed by this risk analysis, ADB will invest in transport infrastructure. ADB is also supporting adaptation and risk-reduction measures needed to increase the resilience of infrastructure to both disaster events and long-term climate change.

Physical investments in roads, ports, and airports integrate resilient design features into all new projects. This includes enough large drainage systems to accommodate increasing rainfall, careful selection of location of maritime structures, and higher and stronger road embankments and breakwaters, as examples. Realignment of roads to higher grounds and coastal protection may be necessary to avoid flooding. ADB is also supporting DMCs in selecting appropriate construction materials that take the climate requirements into consideration.

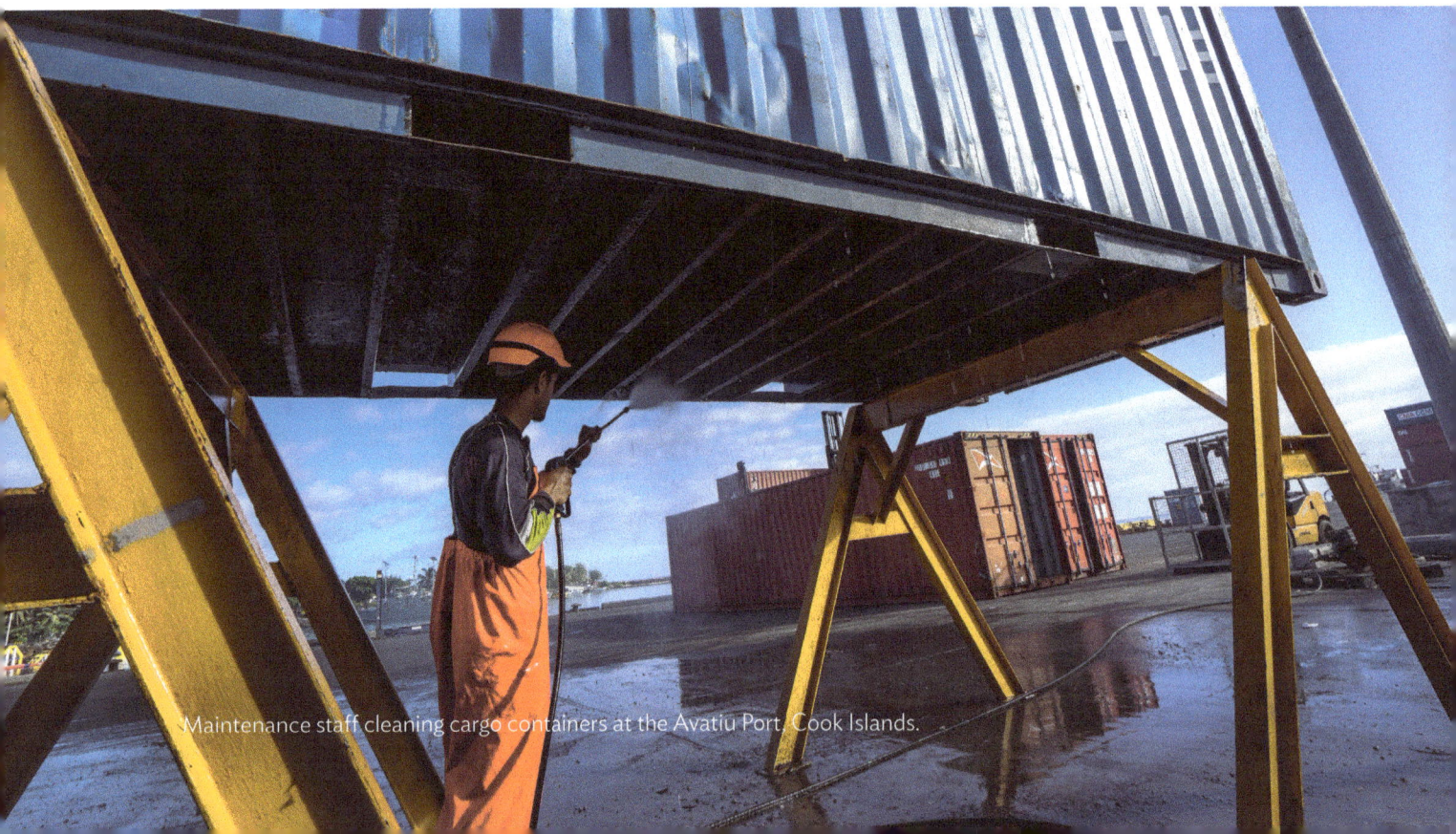

Maintenance staff cleaning cargo containers at the Avatiu Port, Cook Islands.

Transport sector operations have also played a key role in responding to natural disasters. For example, ADB helped Vanuatu reconstruct roads that were damaged by floods during Cyclone Pam in 2015. The project helped restore socioeconomic activity to pre-flood levels, and new roads were constructed under the "build back better" principle.

Regional Cooperation and Integration

Support to the transport sector is fostering deeper regional cooperation and integration by improving connectivity infrastructure and trade logistics. These gains are reducing the cost of doing business, increasing access to international markets, and supporting economic growth. Close coordination through regional facilities, such as PRIF and PSDI, enables donors in the region to identify and act on key investment opportunities—leveraging greater economies of scale and pooled technical resources to achieve greater results on the ground. ADB is helping to identify and reduce trade bottlenecks through regional TA initiatives, by financing relevant infrastructure and by supporting regional communities of best practice. To support deeper regional cooperation, ADB provides TA to the PRIF and PSDI, and a number of thematic initiatives to strengthen dialogue and knowledge sharing among Pacific DMCs. Regional TA initiatives help sector experts in the different Pacific DMCs to share best practices in procurement, implementation, and sustainable infrastructure management practices.

Private Sector Investment and Economic Growth

The Pacific region needs more robust private sector investments in transport infrastructure. However, the business environments in many Pacific DMCs are underdeveloped and lack skilled workers and qualified contractors to implement projects. These constraints discourage the private sector from investing and offering services in many Pacific DMCs. The result has been severely limited private investment in connectivity assets and services across the region.

ADB is supporting the private sector to invest profitably in connectivity infrastructure across the Pacific. It is doing so in two key ways. First, ADB is providing direct support to governments to improve business environments. This includes helping restructure business laws and policies that encourage competition, increase access to finance, and build the skills pools in relevant areas. Second, ADB is supporting the Pacific DMCs to structure public–private partnerships (PPPs), through project preparation support. For instance, ADB is providing transaction advisory services to the Port Moresby International Airport PPP Project. The project will use a PPP scheme where the private sector will operate, rehabilitate, maintain, and expand the airport facilities. ADB also aims to create documents and templates that may be used for future PPPs in the region, and to build local expertise in PPP management and execution in the region. Additionally, ADB is providing capacity building and institutional support for the development of PPP regulation and management. For example, ADB has cofinanced the training of government officials in Samoa as Certified PPP Professionals—Foundation Level.[7]

---

[7]   Financed through the multi donor Asia Pacific Project Preparation Facility.

ADB Approach

All of the Pacific DMCs are small island developing states, which often means that the size of their infrastructure projects is small against international averages. In addition to small economies of scale, the Pacific DMCs experience capacity constraints that affect their ability to plan and manage infrastructure development. These features require a differentiated approach. Close cooperation with other divisions and departments within ADB is necessary to achieve these targets.

The approach is in line with ADB's Strategy 2030 operational priorities, particularly addressing remaining poverty and reducing inequalities; tackling climate change, building climate and disaster resilience, and enhancing environmental sustainability; promoting rural development and food security; strengthening governance and institutional capacity; and accelerating progress in gender equality.

Project readiness. Recognizing the importance of completing detailed project preparatory activities prior to approval, ADB is increasingly using project readiness financing and project development facilities to mobilize consultants at early stages of transport projects in the Pacific. Consultants support DMCs to prepare projects with detailed engineering designs, land surveys, safeguards and due diligence, and even by conducting advance procurement activities. Doing so helps streamline implementation and ensure success once the project is approved. ADB has developed a project readiness financing facility to support this objective, which is being used or prepared in the Federated States of Micronesia, Papua New Guinea, Samoa, Solomon Islands, Tonga, Tuvalu, and Vanuatu.

Quality of infrastructure. Allowing adequate time for civil works ensures the achievement of the targeted outputs without compromising the quality. ADB is encouraging DMCs to prepare conservative timelines for project implementation in the Pacific, considering the often remote locations of project sites and challenges in logistics. ADB designs funding arrangements that carefully take into account the anticipated duration of implementation.

Value for money. ADB will continue to prefer the open competitive bidding method as envisaged in the ADB procurement regulations to procure civil works.[8] Both quality and cost factors are included in evaluation criteria, and quality factors will be increasingly used, where viable, to ensure that the selected bidder is capable of carrying out the works with high quality and within the given timeline and budget.

Cost contingencies. While the focus on improved readiness, conservative timelines, and new procurement guidelines will improve cost controls over projects, ADB will further mitigate the risk of cost overruns by providing sufficient contingencies in all cost estimates. This is necessary to cover the unexpected additional costs, which may occur in the Pacific because of several reasons, including remote locations and adverse weather conditions.

Capacity building. ADB's capacity development support will remain a priority. The range of this support varies widely, including developing technical studies, providing long-term staff and consultants in the DMCs and respective project management units, delivering tailored training to implementation partners (including executing agencies) and other stakeholders across sectors, providing due diligence support,

---

8   ADB. 2017. *Procurement Regulations for ADB Borrowers*. Manila.

and financing relevant services and goods related to infrastructure projects. Increasingly, ADB will seek to deliver long-term capacity support in core sectors, including transport, to ensure sector sustainability. This is particularly important considering the increasing amount of infrastructure assets among DMCs because of ADB's and other development partners' interventions, while capacity remains low and operation and maintenance budgets are insufficient. ADB will continue to support the development of the infrastructure asset management systems in the region.

Innovative financing structures. Sequenced and programmatic lending can encourage deeper engagement of the government in planning, building, managing, and maintaining infrastructure. The multitranche financing facility helps deliver large resource envelopes in a more predictable and flexible way than individual projects. The facility enables ADB to finance larger-ticket transport programs, like highways and airports, in multiple stages and with sequenced targets. This programmatic approach mitigates the issues related to sizable commitment fees for the client and tighter lending headroom for ADB, which are relevant for large-scale stand-alone projects. This modality encourages governments to take ownership of project results and, in turn, to engage more deeply in the development process. Similarly, sector lending encourages close partnerships between ADB, the government, and other development partners to plan sequenced improvements to intermodal transport infrastructure.

ADB's Pacific transport operations leverage innovative financing tools to create larger economies of scale, build capacity alongside physical assets, and streamline project implementation—from preparatory activities to completion. Regional TA encourages knowledge sharing and pooling resources. Programmatic and sector lending—including through the multitranche financing facility—support effective planning for larger, more transformative initiatives. Specialized TA to prepare projects helps streamline implementation.

Road Map

ADB's partnership with the Pacific DMCs is based on the intersection of DMCs' transport sector priorities with ADB's Strategy 2030. A principal objective of ADB support is to help DMCs prepare for and respond to shocks, deliver sustainable services, and support inclusive growth. Support for infrastructure development, including transport, forms a core part of ADB's operational strategy for the region. The following figure demonstrates the strategic linkages as discussed previously.

Figure: Strategic Linkages

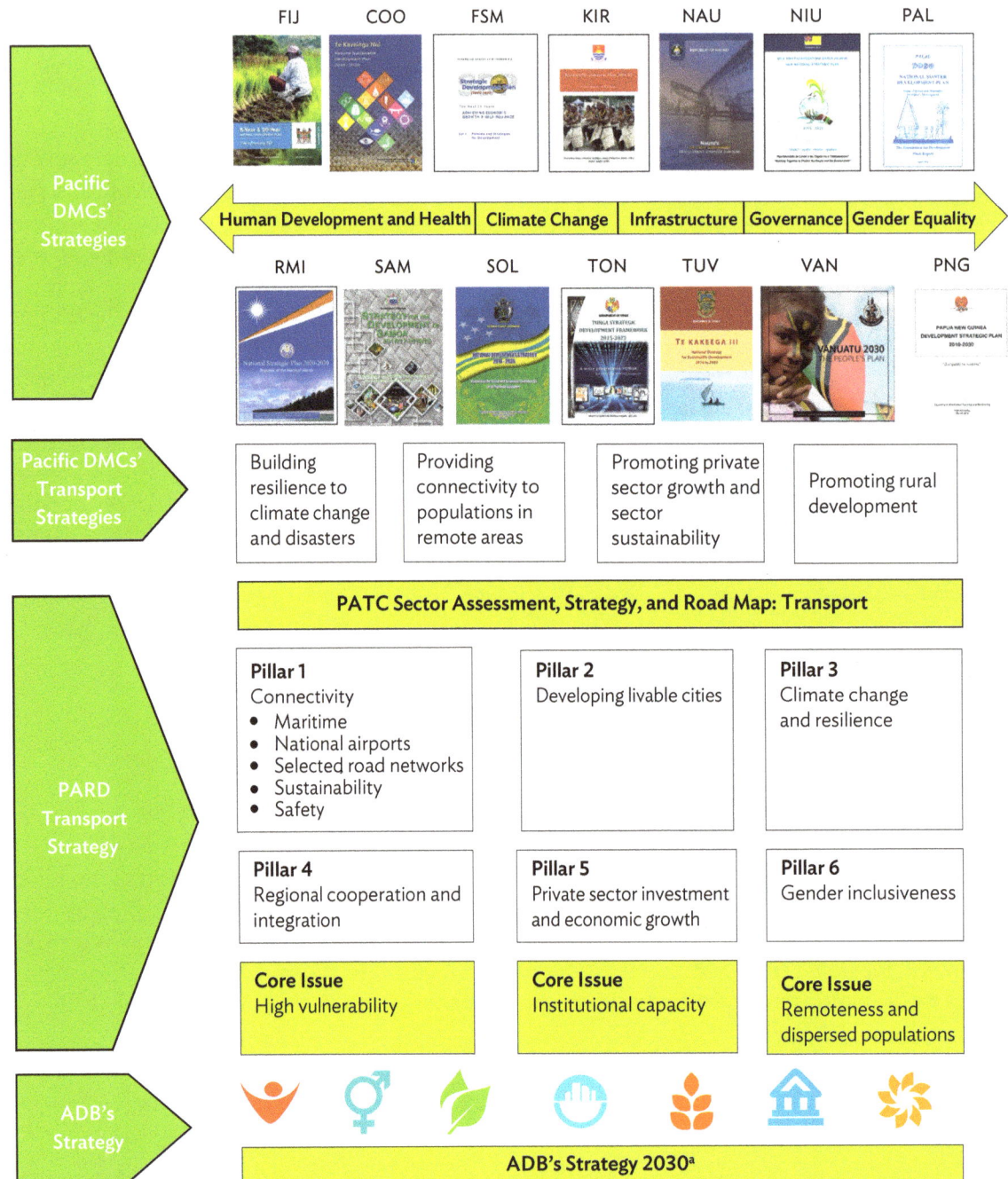

Pacific DMCs' Strategies

FIJ   COO   FSM   KIR   NAU   NIU   PAL

| Human Development and Health | Climate Change | Infrastructure | Governance | Gender Equality |

RMI   SAM   SOL   TON   TUV   VAN   PNG

Pacific DMCs' Transport Strategies

| Building resilience to climate change and disasters | Providing connectivity to populations in remote areas | Promoting private sector growth and sector sustainability | Promoting rural development |

PATC Sector Assessment, Strategy, and Road Map: Transport

PARD Transport Strategy

Pillar 1
Connectivity
- Maritime
- National airports
- Selected road networks
- Sustainability
- Safety

Pillar 2
Developing livable cities

Pillar 3
Climate change and resilience

Pillar 4
Regional cooperation and integration

Pillar 5
Private sector investment and economic growth

Pillar 6
Gender inclusiveness

Core Issue
High vulnerability

Core Issue
Institutional capacity

Core Issue
Remoteness and dispersed populations

ADB's Strategy

ADB's Strategy 2030[a]

ADB = Asian Development Bank, COO = Cook Islands, DMC = developing member country, FIJ = Fiji, FSM = Federated States of Micronesia, KIR = Kiribati, NAU = Nauru, NIU = Niue, PAL = Palau, PARD = ADB Pacific Department, PATC = Transport and Communications Division (Pacific Department), PNG = Papua New Guinea, RMI = Republic of the Marshall Islands, SAM = Samoa, SOL = Solomon Islands, TON = Tonga, TUV = Tuvalu, VAN = Vanuatu

[a]   ADB. 2018. Strategy 2030: *Achieving a Prosperous, Inclusive, Resilient, and Sustainable Asia and the Pacific.* Manila.

Source: ADB.